LYING IN

ALSO BY ELIZABETH METZGER

The Spirit Papers

LYING IN

poems

ELIZABETH METZGER

MILKWEED EDITIONS

Published 2023 by Milkweed Editions
Printed in Canada
Cover design by Mary Austin Speaker
Cover illustration by Mary Austin Speaker
Author photo by Yvette Roman
23 24 25 26 27 5 4 3 2 1
First Edition

Library of Congress Cataloging-in-Publication Data

Names: Metzger, Elizabeth, 1988- author.
Title: Lying in : poems / Elizabeth Metzger.
Other titles: Lying in (Compilation)
Description: First edition. | Minneapolis, Minnesota : Milkweed Editions, 2023. | Summary: "A devastating, vulnerable collection tracing high-risk pregnancy and new motherhood amid grief"-- Provided by publisher.
Identifiers: LCCN 2022030585 (print) | LCCN 2022030586 (ebook) | ISBN 9781639550104 (trade paperback) | ISBN 9781639550111 (ebook)
Subjects: LCGFT: Poetry.
Classification: LCC PS3613.E8946 L95 2023 (print) | LCC PS3613.E8946 (ebook) | DDC 811/.6--dc23/eng/20220711
LC record available at https://lccn.loc.gov/2022030585
LC ebook record available at https://lccn.loc.gov/2022030586

Milkweed Editions is committed to ecological stewardship. We strive to align our book production practices with this principle, and to reduce the impact of our operations in the environment. We are a member of the Green Press Initiative, a nonprofit coalition of publishers, manufacturers, and authors working to protect the world's endangered forests and conserve natural resources. *Lying In* was printed on acid-free 100% postconsumer-waste paper by Friesens Corporation.

For Owen and Willow

CONTENTS

1

2

Everything moves in time with what the belly contains.

—FRIDA KAHLO

1

Lying In

On bed rest desire becomes a sheet.
Let it fall over me
without hands. Let it.

Before I knew I was in danger
I did not get up. After,
when I say how long I lay down
how can I make you understand it was an order?

In bed what time has done to me *is*
what it cannot do
to him. I become the mortal
pregnant with a god, if only he can
be born.

*

Whatever happens don't blame yourself
the ER nurse says when I am

diagnosed with threatened abortion.

She holds my shoulder with one hand.
With the other, crushes a Vicodin.

Can I take that before it's over?

Try to gather yourself says the nurse
so I look for my body everywhere:

The placenta dangles off like fruit about to fall half-mine half-

*

Forget mothers.

The living woman scrapes out the unliving
every month to ferment
and when I bleed I cannot tell the season.

Because California
but not just that.

Because I am careful to forget.

*

I will not stand without a husband.

I will not drink water
without his placing the straw
between my lips.

Watching mobile women round out
is like witnessing the world

have sex
with not-you.

He does love me. *I do I do*
vows turned tantrum

over something like chewing gum

but gifts are fragile bonds
and nothing sticks

to satisfy my sapling doubt.

*

There are moments I wish he would thrust just once
where the half-dead fetus quickens

but then I blink.

Can't you just be gracious? Maybe every woman
has a voice that says this often.

*

Bedridden, a riddle:

the bed does not stay the same throughout.
Body-logged, it sinks
by increments. Even now when I sit on the edge

it is in the shape of my old belly. The bed ridden,
my self rewritten.

*

In labor I have to tell my body many times

letting go is now bringing to life.

But is it too much blood? I say.

The doctor jokes *Are you a virgin?*

I see the head as anticlimactic. *Push. Don't push.*

Beyond the numbness, each contraction.

If there is only enough placenta left to keep one of us

keep him.

*

I know women since the beginning
have healed. What I don't understand

is how the body can hold

a cock again inside it.
I have no choice but to give birth

to everything now, every thought

that comes to mind.
I curse my husband,

sometimes rant against the baby.

I hate most the sound of my own
demanding.

The dead don't hold a grudge

when they're not missed
unless they have the fortune

of coming back.

The moment I first grab our son

to my chest I say
goodbye?

*

My milk, even my voice
holds the scent of his blood

mixed with my time.

I make my kisses heard
like tissue paper on his newborn hair.

And when at four I tickle him

his held breath all over again
stitches us skin to ghost to skin.

In some ways I am gone.

In wildfire ash
I teach our son the alphabet.

O, spin your finger in it.

The world says wean your grief
before it outweighs love.

What if mine does,
what if I put a screen in front

of my boy at noon

to hear myself think.
How should I beg.

What mother.

I lost the baby, I did
even though he lived.

WON EXIT

In one or two lives
I opened the door with the prize
only to find the prize was not worth the life.

I wanted the door.

Brave mahogany door, you be my fortune.
Teach me to understand the cry
in your grain, the suffering circles

by which your tree wisdom is known.

I was superior with handles,
gentle with thresholds. Then, this.

Choices at morning hours I usually skip
but there is a little cashflow of beauty
where there is almost no more water.

And there is not room and light enough
to stand behind the second
and listen anymore—

I am going through the language of me now.

I am flipping open the dictionary of myself
with my tongue
to find your first word.

In the torture of a foyer
doorless for entering, I am entering none.

FIRST WOUND KEPT OPEN

The thought
of all the grass

blown over to one side
hurts me. That wind

can do that. I must have
gotten to him first

though he pushed out against
the pouch in me

I now call soulless.
Of everyone I've met

on earth I always find
they got here first

and will they teach
me their good

reason for staying?
I would discipline

a comet against
my way of leaving,

push it out of sky after
sky and after

every loss on earth
the baby I was

would come back. That's
what it means to be lovable,

to give oneself whole
again whole birth

whole fist whole flower
but only what fits

harmlessly whole
in the mouth.

The baby comes and goes,
comes back to weed me

of my body, feeds my
bald birdies

what's not for me to know.
I had hoped all

my animosity toward men
would lead toward

safety in one who
would wake me before

I hit the wooden world
and rock me there

to say what violence
had not yet come.

We Are Often in Danger of Departing

At first you were fluid and the fluid
held growing.
A napkin tucked

around a nutrient.
Old and imminent,
the spots of the guest within me.

As if two together
could fill a soul like a bathtub,
frequent endings drained your true end

before it could be inflicted.
Touch was better than washing,
even if it was infected.

Then there was just me,
environment for harm. It was over.
It lasted. In every order.

You've Been on Earth So Long Already

All my life all I've wanted was to be myself
and someone else. Not theirs but them.

My shame about this greed made
me hesitant with other children.

I wanted what they wanted, but apart:

I tried to make it, spooned what I could
into shallow mental dishes I stacked
all night and poured through

my neediest hole, which opens only
for medicine or extreme misunderstanding.

My teeth browned from too much
thirst too late.

My eyes bulged from noticing
what I wasn't meant to be.

There was a playground I went to
—and can't take you.

The first thing I did daily
was look for a place to hide, or flee.
There were plenty of gates and wide enough trees

but I stayed off-center, just beyond
the sprinkler's range.

The others played until they snacked
around me. Sometimes they cried.
Sometimes they looked consoled by what they couldn't have.

No not now
The boundary of things. The boundary of time.
I wish this for you—come soon—to be withheld.

They were so freely asking for more world.

Exaggerated Honey

Once there was nobody left to love
a family had me.

My mother made a steeple with her hands
that folded open to reveal no people.

Show me again, I said. Tell me again
not to talk to strangers.

Hospital lights across the street
taught me to stay awake in my own company.

Later I asked strangers to take my hand
across. I used to think I hated where I came from

and would leave, that children elsewhere
found safety in freedom, but there is no fire

anywhere I am capable of rubbing.
I am not mother enough to bear

creating my own heat, not human enough
to come close to what's untouchable.

Call me complaint. Call me *honey you exaggerate.*
When my family laughs in the hallway

I laugh with my hair thrown back to the ground
like I understand them. Just to be answered,

I take it as seriously as the dead
or a bridge to nowhere. But what loss on earth

would I honestly like to stay for? And life
is no better, thank god. It also keeps us.

Picture of the Floating World

The wave said *Want.*
The wave said *Childless.*

Child, I bend around you
like a boat.

If you live
do not blame the wave.

When you grow into my mother
do not blame the wave.

When you grow to hate me
let it be one rogue moment repeated.

Though you can't help but love me again,
do not put me in the ground.

Nor take me out.
By then I will be a new corpse

snowing
over Mount Fuji

and you will be the solid water
un-arriving.

With your love final and pushing
me earthward

when I am dead
and you are dying

you will have been through me.
Not still.

Patient Mentality

I closed my eyes and looked up
at the ceiling I knew would be the last distance
I would ever see but not yet

and the voluntary nature of staying alive seemed
obvious
against the red ladder of my body

NOT MY CHILD

Here where dark cherries grow up from the ground
and have not been penetrated
by time or branches

I wake on a hip that has fallen asleep
and there you are
with a fully grown family

sledding inward
down one mud-caked hill.
Were I your child

I would be your children
several ladders
with slightly different oil-spills

undermining my bases.
I'd be slipping and swaying
beneath your capacities

and on one too-long night
you would bleed from my holes
and be fine.

Dead so early before sunup?
you'd say, literally planting a kiss
in my absence

like a weed too petty
to rip out. I wish
I could tell why my body appalls me

even though you have thrived.
Nobody died
but that's just the luck of it.

THE WITCHING HOUR

In life
if I could say for sure

what I have loved
there would be

no tunnel needed
for any inner

or earthly transport.
Everywhere

I turned
there would appear

only the blinding clubs
of the sun

and when I thought
of escape

I would thank
a dead man

for my thoughts
and lick

through his navel
all my sweet unknowable

time. He would be lanky
and love and

unlove me.
I would not worry

about our undoing,
about survivals.

I would get up from bed
and be gone

with the kit of the careless.
In my confusion

I would have a child.
I already did. I did

him a fatal injury
bringing him here.

They handed him
out of my body

onto my body.
When he cried I misled him

with joy, beckoned
by something that knew

my hands better than I,
toward the soft spot

of earth. It was not
childhood. I'm a mother now

and I can promise
under the grown breast

the heart is still changeable
that far down.

When I grieve
he plays with the salt.

He hangs on the
faulty edge

of my face. I have him uneven.
I have him to hold

my life open
like a towel

and take my pains
then feed me one star

on a fork and say
no big deal.

MOSES, NEW YORK

There was a boat on the pond
but no water. The water had sacrificed

itself for your brutal thirst. Goodbye,
cowboys. Goodbye, not knowing

to speak.

The boat is ready for me, baby.
Enough with the reeds and the motherless.

One singular horn
will turn your face purple.

A leaf blower may take your breath away.

But the boat here is always
and human. It floats on nothing.

All the surfaces for floating
and reflecting are gone. What good is

what passes through us but clouds?

There is a branch overhead
as if there were birds. And I would rather

show you than go.

2

WELCOME

His being. Also his leaving.

He will come and be
lost, a thin mighty friend

curled in the pillowy
none-left

of my ovary. At the first stroke
of red he must ride

my tubes empty
to find me. Look,

all my blundered life

you loved me more
than I could ever love you.

If the one I miss most
were to come

like the light of the none-left
like the light of the not-yet

I would ride
and ride without sorrow.

THE WHOLE WAY

You will walk through the worst
forest like any tree
toward a glowing yellow
hole in the ground you would
almost have to step over if you were
just human.
It will be a bird why not
I cannot fly so I glow
and if that's sorrow you
scoop it into your fat palm
where the lines of a lifetime
belong to you alone
and leave you alone at both ends.
The bird guides you where you don't know
you're going then wilder
in my safety
you ask the bird not me
What do you lose by protecting
Who would ever sleep

WITH WAYWARD MOTION

The wind parted me.
Wind from nowhere.

It did not get up
from its snoring carriage

or offer me a bottle
of near future.

It did not cry
so much as moan

into the mouth of a
passing monument.

There goes my self
with invisible scissors

narrowing my loves,
dusting the pollen

off spring like another
previous opportunity.

We argued about what
could be unconditional.

We forgot to pay.
We forgot to die

was also our only chance
to be infinitive

in real time. One of us
loved the other like

an instrument that
would not ever again

be played
though it was perfectly

strung and oiled.
Mother love came up

and of course children
but what about their

scrotums and egg sacs.
Could we already adore

those in extremis?
The wind was all over

my face reminding me
of my other affairs:

The impermissible.
The impermanent.

The sex between all
who already possessed

themselves and were
satisfied, not by me.

EARLY RISING

when the earth took away my fires
I sighed in bodies

I mean the sighs had limbs and trunks
and as with bodies

some were living
some not
some almost
or almost headless

like the ember I thought was over
that blew up into a planet

mostly water and everything connected was a kinder island

which did not betray the aims of water

or bury what my hands have buried
or nurture
what your hands have warmed
then scorched

before I took
away my earth

my earths were buried
and I rubbed apart their pieces
for your fire

put me out
put me where I don't forgive by heart

LAST OF KIN

We came with others where
we came alone.

Though it was world we never saw it whole.

There were seasons. There were senses.

Time called to space but the phone was
off the hook, old phone.

What else was instantaneous

the air
how we destroyed it.

God, or our last child
made to make ourselves believe in...
an excuse from language.

What we couldn't know:
how paper tears most completely once torn a little.

We were moving when we thought we were most still.

We had nowhere else to go.

First Anniversary

The fog makes a uterus

last one
we can occupy
together since we cannot

occupy each other yet
again.

You'd probably prefer to sneak back into me

very still, swollen
with a rural vestige of you.

We lie apart inside
a soon contracted room.

For once it holds us

up to dark, a year of poisons
and power cord horizons.

I see you entering the driveway
ready to bring me to
the next *this* world.

For a moment it's not you
with the keys

but a foggy boy closed up in wonder
not seeing me

into the house
and then you say, who's here?

ULTRASOUND

I brought a weather with me

but it was not expectable
that he would stay this long in spite of rust

on a metal mountain above a desert
I've never been to

Don't pretend
it is free to watch parts move

Where a train breaks down
he goes pushing it along without anything changed or missing

Who is that dancing in rare lightning over there

It is a lot like his life will be
not for him

for me for me for me

A Birth Interrupted On and Off by the World

The unborn depend on the love of
non-mothers. Remember to orgasm alone

in their dreams. Alone in dreams
I watched the flowers fuck.

Because the dreamer cannot be seen
I was touched (even in dreams)
by nothing.

Guest House

There is the ghost of a child in me.

It longs to die, so afraid of living
it gives up a little while of my life:

a friend, a city, the election, maybe the child.

The ghost of the child I have now
clings to the nursery.

You are early, I say, *he's alive.*

Worse, the ghost hardens
like furniture cluttering and dividing

the most spacious rooms
while its longing goes about the earth-of-me chores.

Weeding where the child can't pass.

For My Mother Wanting Children

All this breeze and nothing will be moved.
I don't blame you.

The wasted life still carries a self through it

one boulder easily displaced
on top of another
with a fluctuant light

seeming to displace me. Somebody besides you
made you never enough.

Made me superhumanly the same
as what you thought you lost.

There is wreckage

in wishing for new life more
than waving back at those who hummed
away their moment.

Once or twice I dreamed you asked me
to open some incision
and tuck myself in. The worst part was

I had to fit. The best part was you were a body.

Inmate of Happiness

Because you were born with your knees
tied together under you
you are bound to need your hands
and resent my knees.

Because you were born with and without knees
your face remains close to the ground
to scrutinize the methods
the medics use to unhook them:

they splint your legs to planks,
numb each knee with a balm
that makes you feel you are flying
through stone. Now you crouch

ready to doubt, blinking because
it is your body's to blink.
You smile, invincibly obscured.
From any closer I couldn't take you whole

so you imagine your hands luring
my knees into both sides of your mouth
and open your smile
into a needy room—

behind your teeth, a person of pity
mired in thick shame.
Because you were born to be happy
you would skin and uncap

the knee of a good giant
to make yourself a helmet
to guard your sorry brain, but
you cannot get up off those knees.

MID-SUPPER

I am moving on, where am I?

Between mother and child: let me
pass the plate forever.

They have sat and
gotten up from the table for the same
solitary meal.

For what I am giving up, help me follow
how I used to get by:

undressed pretzel-style
pulled back the checkered curtain

for the window to sing
with the closeness of cold.

When the song is exhausted
let me blow out the
mother left over.

So this way is forward.

3

GODFACE

Once I sat straining to keep you whole
when Max said

look up
that high window was made to keep you aware
of an exit you can't access
but will be forced through.
You will want the exact pain then
you would die of now.

                    He said
look down
the mosaic tiles are not just a cold
assembly of random glass.
They are what god is, individual for each
of us, a face designed
with all our dead
in novel arrangements—
friends, ancestors, strangers,
even what has not yet lived.

So you are here, and there still,
making up my godface,
and if by winter you raise your eyes
into this dimension,
you will already have renamed the places
my body touches
through this one-room world.

THE IMPOSSIBILITY OF CROWS

Your death has just begun but it is not
spoken of, it speaks
in odd weathers like a second first love

as if the snow could fall for real here
as if you would deign to visit me through sun.

There are no directions

the edges of your death are smudged and round
like ash or a watch
whose accuracy is the least of its worth.

There is no clear ill will
there is no bronzy heaven.

You will come to me instead
though I never came to you
won't you?

It's not too late yet.
There hasn't been blood or sex
not even the spirit or
splinted ambition.

Today I will stay for
just the last unafraid adoring avalanche of you

as if my life had wound itself up
and let go with yours

a made metal crow
acting born

choosing its cracktime
then tiptoeing off your branch of the world.

WRONG DISTANCE

Don't you miss me as if I were dead?

That's how you'd like to be loved.

To be forgotten then
remembered in a god's red fleece
too big for either of us.

What would you do
if the world started gathering
like snow
shoveled by your own demise
and I was nowhere, sheets tucked in
(hospital corners), for
several elusive afternoons.

I have been at rest
for years myself, hearing humans
I've made and will make, domesticating.
Meanwhile, you've earned birthday tea
and my loving surveillance.

I was certain such darkness as ours
could be lit
by the right explosives
at the wrong distance.

Just before my flight back
you were passing cattails from hand
to hand to demonstrate

what sister-love could have been.

The End that Followed

When you died you died—
what could I do for your words?

Hold them in the jewel roaster
and pile on one more most glorious log?

Between gravity and fire who wins?
If the embers came back down to their match

something would have to harden
but that doesn't mean permanence.

It is through disappearing again
that you become tunnels

that you move others on.
Sideways ruby newborn in the earth

someone mistook me for blood
or the eardrum of a paranoid lover.

Someone was always singing in your sleep.
Words, then fire, please don't check

up on life anymore. I didn't know
one death could keep happening

and then keep happening
or others would be going so soon.

By morning you were alive again
and I was no kind of mother.

MERCY LATER

There is a green chair I don't belong to.
I keep it in the middle of every room.

Departures remind me
I never traveled far for anyone but myself.
Hi, hi you say to the green chair.

I ran today with you sort of in my arms
toward the ambulance, full of appetite
for emergency   *we oh we oh*

we were giddy in the siren sun.
Turns out a woman had just died crossing here.

Suddenly everyone including you earned half my hate.
A bird I once used in a poem
whom I never thought again of.

I can't say I ever enjoyed anything
except coming home
                          to the green

in the middle of my rooms.

VERISIMILITUDE

A too-human angel doesn't leave me alone.
He stands in the neighbor's yard
facing his hedges
so that you literally have to creep onto the property
to see his judgmental wings
covered in Post-its scrawled
with all the hateful thoughts of the world
in felt-tip cobalt.
As I nudge the stroller around the corner,
my son just finally asleep,
I imagine his adult knuckles hating around
some nonexistent pen
then finding his keys in deep pockets
and braving home
where I'll never have been.
Sometimes I turn in and read one
on the shorn dry good enough grass
so that maybe that night I will have forgiven another person.

ALMOST ONE

I am no longer twinned.
The reflection of my room in the window is so convincing,

it goes on,
the placement of furniture identical
& appreciated & I am not visible looking out.

To surpass the reflection.
To hunt the suburban night for wheels.

There is another mind here—

It will start to ask me how things work.
I dread it.

Doors don't just open & close,
people leave them open people leave them closed.

When you ask me one night far away
like a searchlight across the underworld
would I come get you, give you life all over,
I say   *I would.*

              I say it easily because this night
the arts have stopped &
if there are voices
demanding my presence, they are still expecting
another birth.

So I Finally Slept

At first I was afraid
of what felt like mutual need

but soon his initial comfort
was like cornsilk

stripped with the ear
and compelled to the beautiful

dead. He had evolved too
he said, as any irregularity

in a mammal and had crafted
forever into an answer of milk

from his bodilessness
that no one would drink.

I showed him what still
swayed inside me and

how grueling it is to harbor
someone's thirst

rather than the drink.
He didn't mind that I had not

believed him. Like a sleeved arm
into an ocean suddenly full

of another power of movement
and then with all suddenness

revoked he put me to sleep
with a simple asymmetrical gesture.

No patting or sweet partings
just the exponential side

of his face on my face and he
never came back for me faithful.

THE FLAT CHAPEL

There's a wall that grows in a sunflower field
and calls to worship nobody at all.
Everyone is sorrier than last time
in their homes closed around a divine intervention.
Who will save the field from the bodies
blown in from the station, tickets
spilling from muscle?
The suicidal geese
whose migration only the sickliest children track
from their cots, who will save them?
The wall has a hole toward forgetting.
I have pressed myself up to it
as a clumsy well-off child and again
in my late rebel weakness. Oh lucky-ass window
you see the whole passage of time
with no duties, not having to doubt the cloud
or the vine. And the wall says
Looking through me is not worship.
What vision can be given?
What visible is true?

ONE MORE DAY

I kept rolling away rocks

to let the plumes pass—why
was I here again

testing for heat
with the back of my hand

Things had been going hellishly for a long while
which meant many were making me hate

A voice I couldn't place called out
maybe the fire will save the house

—did it mean *spare*

There had been another flare-up
I welcomed the staticky cry

It did not ask for my help, and I did not offer

I was counting down the days to a new conception
instead of

hosing down the straw homes of my neighbors

Ash landed on my cheek
it was a ladybug—

There is a lot about others I don't remember
Outlived an interest

What is the point, the voice said

of knowing you are not the only one
burning yourself down

EVERY CHILD ALONE

The world closed. The family
went back to its origins.
Didn't they move away finally
as they promised?

Here in my future, is this
the hotel you told me about?

It is summer I guess.
I haven't been outside since winter.
I am a child
still of extremeness.

I run into the arms of a man.
I never even loved him in real life.

He fathers me in a dream.
I know he has to stand for me
his face a clear wish for beginning.
He is my emptiest thing.

My brain shrinks in daylight.
My fingers degenerate so early.

The past is moving, I am young already.

My mother speaks her old German
she never taught us a word of——

consonants of a house settling.
We never lived in a house.

If I feel sure
I will never understand her
she can feel the same about me, she says, and adore me.

What does it mean you regret all of it?
We tried. We could not have talked longer.

She says I have never known violence,
and I remember

I knew you. Oh my god do I know you.

4

As Long As They Want

Back I go into a body carelessly
groomed, like a plant

it conceived me

alone
with the root of aloneness

then was blown
toward a mother more consuming
than mine.

Between departures I had children
and between children
mothers.

Both are my cohorts now.

Having sedated my hands
again in time

I fly home for the chance
to watch mothers
play as children

for as long as they want

bouncing the quietest balls
on the heads of their children to be.

The God Incentive

He kept me through childhood.
There was a reason
he kept me from sin like a biscuit
warming in the oven.

It's okay, I tell the rain, to keep him a theory
but bring him down
once in a while.

It's okay to be honest or selfish
but find the spot where you sink
a little into the velvet stadium seat
of secrets other secrets
have rubbed away.

See I have been alone and didn't know it
waiting on the inside glass
of a trafficked world
where one mistrust passes another
with a long yellow horn
that no hand can quiet.

Something other than science
is pressing down on my night watch
saying sing here
instead of signing off this hour.
Ride the hard part,
that is the good part. As many
holy animals know.

SEX DREAM

What part of lying still
left room for missing you? I missed the floor,
I missed letting the shower hit my stomach
without consequence. Then
I missed the nurse.

I did not miss violence, not passion.
I still had those, if hidden.

Never longed for a moment to last.
Never thought of the night
your hand
brought out the wet proof of my life.

I was for the first time neutral,
the only angel of wait,
all the weeks one page
I was graceful at turning. Will you ever open me
the old way and not be wrecked,
I did not expect to ever ask you.

MARRIAGE

You want to know what I actually love?
It is the mind I don't have access to
Like a flower cut and placed on a kitchen table,
Looking more like a human body than
It could in the field with its kind. What does species matter,
Things die please remind me
When I say I don't feel anything, and then
It is better for them to be broken down
Again, a powder once fertile
And original. Now
In need of none of those powers.
Let me try saying it again, I don't feel anything
So something can die
Further down, yes like that
Like the last time I came across
A flower that wasn't planted. We don't have to
Make it actual, no more wild purpose of hands.

ROACH

The quickness of living.
The quickness of wanting to kill something.
Forget dreams, they attack me and
I welcome their landings
as I'd welcome a gas mask
filled with all our unsayable
thoughts. Kiss me again
without being asked
or asking if I still love. How
to possess an exoskeleton,
earth kitchen, shiny
brown god's house, guts hollowed?
I don't know
what marriage means at 2 a.m.
with six or seven roaches vying
for my mouth and other
openings. If someone handed me a
microscope I might wake up.
A microphone, I might stop
and listen. If you're not breathing
on your own
by the middle of this lifetime
it isn't worth the privilege of lifting
your feet. I made you. I make to lay myself
out like a glue trap,
safe. The exterminator says
they are checking
out the new smell of our baby
in the holy sliver where

our bodies don't touch.
I don't think he would hurt them
now that he understands
them. I don't think you would
hurt me, though I've killed you
many times, either.

On a Clear Night

I have broken our heart again. I have made the animal noise
the animal, you know I make up
what I don't know. I used to think that was resilience.

If I could speak with an earlier you
I would say have I told you what will happen to us,
and you would laugh trusting I knew.

All I would have to do is read, really read in front of you.
Do you see my relationship to my face?
I wish to pull myself out of it. Of course I can't

but I love wishing. No matter how much I tell you
there is as much I cannot tell you.

Mother Nothing

You were placed like wings are placed
as if they'll never be needed to leave with

but then you were born

and each time I unwrap your diaper
I consider every feeling you will hide from me.

When I wipe you I am touched with envy.

*

You made the water you broke.
You made me sicker than I could stand

to live a little longer.
For every night there is another night I've missed.

Maybe it is my ambivalence
about being outlasted.

Whenever you are in your crib
my life feels final, or like it has never been.

*

You do not speak still.

Orange growing bitter within its skin,
why would you speak?

Alone in time
pretending you can't rot because you are held in.

Each word you say is still just pulp in your voice.

*

All night your long-into-life silence distracts me.

                Are you there?

Pleasure is the uterus contracting emptiness.
Since you came, it asks

*What will ever be as good as holding
a new life?*

*

If you were my lover I would beg you to speak *speak*

I practice a voice that will make you adult
but you are not my lover   then
you are the mother I was always after

lie back

desire is no longer inside me,
you are my

                  uncertainties

*

so who am I if not your
practice man?

*

I could say your lack of babbling is not a drought
but the river taking itself back.

Ignore my mouth moving sound out toward you.

You shouldn't be accountable
for what I make.

Reach for the bars instead,
pull yourself along my night mind.

All children grow into questions.

You end
but never as I left you.

Daughter as Myself

She feeds her rabbits.
Without their mouths they eat. Ah
their instincts are taken away.
Why twitch why hop when buckled when this world
is choosing between buckles.

Eyeing the fake moss that grows over the kitchen gate
she used to want safe want safe more
than wanting at all.
What would she do with one tooth.
What would she do with a substance to crunch only
in the same spot repeatedly.

Taste no taste.
Pull a sheet over your tongue if you have to.
Invent a tongue
for the carrot. This meal is purely
for passing through.

What Are the Chances

I go home to my dead
try to want less

the communion with my closest candle.

Forget the fire I have done fire.
I haven't burned anything without planning.

There is a man that stays away in me.

He has already missed most of my life.
He never finds words

and is either too old or too young.

Try to go back to shy smiles
slow appetite

a dress that floats up on a bus

through the daydreams of strangers.
With a lantern—that kind of child.

Was it mine, my daydream

awareness, even then it was the awareness
that made me more despicable.

Some were wrongful I'm sure

they did want more than
to pinch my cheeks and

rode the elevator just to find me

and some were caretakers as they claimed,
if only I had let them adore me.

DESIRE

It is for you I put the children to bed.

Or, come. I will keep the house awake for you.

The floor is fluttering with tongues.
I step through and you step after me

                                  laughing,

these are toys.

                Isn't it obvious how we've changed?

I have no more use for pure feeling.
You escape directly behind my head.

Little vitrines in the closed museums
not being looked at

                      I would die to be their objects.

The children left me.
You say they came.

What could you possibly do for my body
when I am in two

                separate rooms,
                breathing?

NOTES

Lying In is a cultural practice of bed rest or confinement that occurs before, during, and after giving birth. It traditionally encompasses the first forty days after birth. Etymologically, the word "quarantine" also refers to a period of forty days.

The epigraph of this book comes from a rhyme Frida Kahlo wrote on the back of her painting "Without Hope." The translation is taken from *Frida: A Biography of Frida Kahlo* by Hayden Herrera.

Picture of the Floating World:
   "Ukiyo-e," translated as "Pictures of the Floating World," refers to a nineteenth-century style of Japanese art. One famous example is Katsushika Hokusai's "The Great Wave."

Godface:
   "Max" refers to the poet Max Ritvo. Everything he says here is said posthumously. In other words, made up. Max's death coincided with my first pregnancy. Several poems in *Lying In* are for Max.

The Impossibility of Crows:
   This title comes from Number Thirty-Two of *The Zurau Aphorisms* by Franz Kafka, translated by Michael Hofmann: "The crows like to insist that a single crow is enough to destroy heaven. This is incontestably true, but it says nothing about heaven, because heaven is just another way of saying: the impossibility of crows." I dedicate this poem to Lucie Brock-Broido.

Daughter as Myself:

This title owes a debt to Emily Dickinson's phrase "Doctor as yourself," from a letter to Elizabeth Holland.

Acknowledgments

Thank you to the editors of the following journals and anthologies in which poems from *Lying In* have appeared, sometimes in earlier versions: *American Poetry Review, The Common, Conjunctions, Guernica, Laurel Review, Los Angeles Review, Narrative Magazine, The Nation, New Yorker, Paris Review, Plume, Poem-a-Day, Poetry Magazine, Poetry is Bread, Poetry Northwest, SAND,* and *Yale Review.*

Infinite thanks to everyone at Milkweed, especially Daniel Slager, Bailey Hutchinson, Joy Katz, Joanna Demkiewicz, Joey McGarvey, Broc Rossell, Meilina Dalit, Tijqua Daiker, Morgan LaRocca, and Mary Austin Speaker who gave this book its dream home and made the publishing experience itself a source of inspiration. To make this book with you has been the great joy of my life, and in more ways than I can express here, the most meaningful return to life.

A special thank you to Mark Bibbins, Jeffrey Levine, Kristina Marie Darling, and everyone at Tupelo Press for including versions of twenty of these poems in my chapbook *Bed.* To everyone at the *Los Angeles Review of Books* over the years, especially my co-editor Callie Siskel, Medaya Ocher, Boris Dralyuk, and Gabrielle Calvocoressi. To the School of the Arts community at Columbia University, and my students there and elsewhere. To everyone at University of Massachusetts Press, in particular Dara Barrois/Dixon and James Haug, and to Justin Boening and Devon Walker-Figueroa of Horsethief Books, who first brought my work to an audience.

Tremendous thanks to Kaveh Akbar, Dorothea Lasky, and Katie Peterson for offering their generous words. Thanks to all my teachers, mentors, dear friends, and family, including those who are still very much with me from the other side: Lucie

Brock-Broido, Max Ritvo, Jean Valentine, and Richard Howard. To my first teachers from The Nightingale-Bamford School, Julie Whitaker and Christine Schutt, who made language a way of life. To Forrest Gander, for bearing with me and buoying me at Brown and beyond. To Alice Quinn, for her wisdom throughout. A deep bow to Timothy Donnelly for his brilliant eye and eternal oculus.

Always thanks to Max Ritvo, my daemon, and his radiant circle, especially Riva Ariella Ritvo-Slifka, his devoted mother. To my family—Metzger, Attanasio, and chosen others. Thank you to the poets I admire who have read and offered invaluable feedback to me as I wrote these poems, including L.A. Johnson, Austen Leah Rose, Catherine Pond, Meghan Maguire Dahn, Richard Quigley, Margaret Ross, and many others unnamed in this moment. Thank you to Lia Kohl and Daniel Loedel for musing with me across genres. Thank you, Estelle Shane, for unconditional love and endless listening. Thank you to Yvette Roman for seeing me. Thank you to my nurse-sister Lisa Park and the entire medical team that cared for me during my pregnancies. To my children, Owen and Willow, who have made me and continue to remake me as a person and poet. To my husband Dan Attanasio, who sees every poem as soon as it is born. Without your heart and brain, this book would not be alive.

Yvette Roman

ELIZABETH METZGER is the author *The Spirit Papers*, winner of the Juniper Prize for Poetry, and the chapbook *Bed*, winner of the Sunken Garden Chapbook Poetry Prize. Her poems have been published in the *New Yorker*, *Paris Review*, *Poetry*, *American Poetry Review*, *The Nation*, and Poem-a-Day. Her essays have been published in *Boston Review*, *Guernica*, *Conjunctions*, *PN Review*, and Literary Hub, among others. She is a poetry editor at the *Los Angeles Review of Books*.

milkweed
EDITIONS

Founded as a nonprofit organization in 1980, Milkweed Editions is an independent publisher. Our mission is to identify, nurture, and publish transformative literature, and build an engaged community around it.

Milkweed Editions is based in Bdé Óta Othúŋwe (Minneapolis) within Mní Sota Makhóčhe, the traditional homeland of the Dakhóta people. Residing here since time immemorial, Dakhóta people still call Mní Sota Makhóčhe home, with four federally recognized Dakhóta nations and many more Dakhóta people residing in what is now the state of Minnesota. Due to continued legacies of colonization, genocide, and forced removal, generations of Dakhóta people remain disenfranchised from their traditional homeland. Presently, Mní Sota Makhóčhe has become a refuge and home for many Indigenous nations and peoples, including seven federally recognized Ojibwe nations. We humbly encourage our readers to reflect upon the historical legacies held in the lands they occupy.

milkweed.org

Milkweed Editions, an independent nonprofit publisher, gratefully acknowledges sustaining support from our Board of Directors; the Alan B. Slifka Foundation and its president, Riva Ariella Ritvo-Slifka; the Amazon Literary Partnership; the Ballard Spahr Foundation; *Copper Nickel*; the McKnight Foundation; the National Endowment for the Arts; the National Poetry Series; and other generous contributions from foundations, corporations, and individuals. Also, this activity is made possible by the voters of Minnesota through a Minnesota State Arts Board Operating Support grant, thanks to a legislative appropriation from the arts and cultural heritage fund. For a full listing of Milkweed Editions supporters, please visit milkweed.org.

Interior design by Tijqua Daiker and Mary Austin Speaker
Typeset in Nassim Latin

Designed by Titus Nemeth, Nassim is a contemporary typeface
with a calligraphic heritage. Nemeth's typefaces focus on Arabic
among other multilingual designs, thus Nassim has a vast array
of features that allows for a wide range of applications.